# SANJEEV KAPOOR'S
# SIMPLY VEGETARIAN
### Recipes for the Indian Kitchen

*Sweets & Desserts*

# SANJEEV KAPOOR'S
# SIMPLY VEGETARIAN
## Recipes for the Indian Kitchen

# *Sweets & Desserts*

In association with Alyona Kapoor

Popular Prakashan

POPULAR PRAKASHAN PVT. LTD.

© 2004 by Sanjeev Kapoor

First Published 2004

(3881)

ISBN - 81-7991-133-0

PRINTED IN INDIA
By Thomson Press (I) Ltd.
18/35 Milestone, Delhi Mathura Road, Faridabad (Haryana)
and Published by Ramdas Bhatkal
for Popular Prakashan Pvt. Ltd.

Exclusively Distributed by : Impulse Marketing

# Dedication

To all the lovers of authentic
food whose enthusiasm makes us
dig deeper into the
Khazana of Khana, and come up
with what is best
and most precious in cuisine.

# Acknowledgements

A.I. Kazi

Afsheen Panjwani

Anand Bhandiwad

Mrs. Lata Lohana & Capt. K. K. Lohana

Debashish Mukherjee

Dhiraj Bolur

Drs. Meena & Ram Prabhoo

Ganesh Pednekar

Harpal Singh Sokhi

Jijesh Gangadharan

Jyotsna & Mayur Dvivedi

Kishore Roy

Mallika Shetty

Manish Anand

Namita Pusalkar

Namrata & Sanjiv Bahl

Neelima Acharya
Neena Murdeshwar
Pallavi Sharma
Pooja & Rajeev Kapoor
Priti Surve
Rajeev Matta
Rutika Samtani
Sanjay Bakshi
Satish Parab
Shivani Ganesh
Smeeta Bhatkal
Swapna Shinde
Tripta Bhagattjee
Vinayak Gawande

# Note to the Readers

Let's spin a sugary web around the world! It would be a much better place to live in. Those who travel around would vouch for the fact that there is one specific sweet or dessert that makes that particular region famous. In our country, come winters and practically every home in Punjab will make *garma garam Gajar Halwa*. If that is not enough they will entertain unexpected guests with piping hot *Gulab Jamuns* bought from the local *halwai*. The quality is superb, needless to say, and we have both recipes here for you to enjoy making them, savouring them and sharing them.

India is world famous for its *mithais*. What we do not realize is that there are some assembled desserts that can give the best of the best international desserts a run for their money! Riffle through to *Khubani ka Meetha*. That's proof enough. I have innovated an excellent *Mixed Fruit Kheer*, which is nutritious too. Then, for old times' sake, *Moongdal*

*Halwa* too can grace the dessert bowls.

But as our vision expands we look at some international sweet serves such as *Strawberry Cheesecake*, *Toffee Apple* and *Chocolate Brownies*. These are as accepted by the Indian palate as is Indian food in toto by foreigners!

Be it a light dessert at the end of a heavy meal or be it a heavy dessert at the end of a light meal, the universal law of dessert being the final course holds true. Well, in India, something sweet does not necessarily have to be eaten at the end of the meal. One could open a snack tin and munch through a couple of *Mawa Gujiyas* or pack a few *Motichoor Laddoos* in our child's tiffin. Not to be left behind is the *Choco Coconut Laddoo*, which is a new *avatar* of the traditional coconut sweet.

I feel desserts should not only tempt the palate, they should please the eye too. They could be poetic postscripts to your meal and some preparations in this book will prove themselves true. You will find your old favourites here, alongside some more unusual recipes, which are destined to become your new favourites. There are goodies that can fill up your snack tins to the brim. Hence take a while to try them out for when the festive season comes you can serve homemade goodies. Most of the recipes have been portioned for a family of four people, but they can easily be halved for two or doubled for eight.

Desserts are like the last act of a finely constructed play or like the ending chapter of a book. They might be a reflection of the meal but will definitely leave the imagination wandering. From a creamy *basundi* to a fluffy sweet *pulao*, from *phirnis* to cool *kulfis*, desserts might be the last course to be served but are certainly not the least!

# CONTENTS

Boondi and Bread Pudding ....................................................21

Santra ni Basundi................................................................23

Badami Besan ke Laddoo ....................................................24

Black Currant Kulfi with Mango Salsa ..............................25

Khubani ka Meetha..............................................................27

Chanar Payesh .....................................................................28

Basoondi ..............................................................................33

Motichoor Laddoo ..............................................................34

Chandrakala .........................................................................35

Zafrani Pulao .......................................................................37

Kalakand...............................................................................38

Dudhi Halwa .......................................................................39

Strawberry Cheese Cake .....................................................40

Lavang Latika .......................................................................42

Scoopy Fruit Caramel..........................................................44

Chocolate Walnut Burfi ............................................................ 46
Kaju Katli .............................................................................. 48
Ukdiche Modak ...................................................................... 51
Rawa Naral Laddoo ................................................................. 53
Fruit Kababs with Black Currant Dip ....................................... 54
Date Rolls .............................................................................. 57
Moong Dal Halwa ................................................................... 58
Khajoori Shahi Tukra .............................................................. 61
Ada Pradhaman ...................................................................... 63
Gur aur Badam ki Phirni ......................................................... 65
Choco Coconut Laddoo ........................................................... 67
Gil-e-Firdaus .......................................................................... 68
Mixed Fruit Kheer .................................................................. 70
Toffee Apple ........................................................................... 72
Shrikhand ............................................................................... 74
Surti Ghari ............................................................................. 75
Sandesh .................................................................................. 81

Strawberry and Pista Phirni ..................................... 82

Rasmalai .................................................................. 84

Suji aur Badam ka Halwa ........................................ 86

Matar ki Kheer ....................................................... 88

Amrakhand .............................................................. 91

Peas and Prunes Kheer ............................................ 92

Semiya Payasam ...................................................... 94

Steamed Date Buns ................................................. 95

Burfiwali Chocolate Phirni ...................................... 97

Mawa Gujiya ........................................................... 98

Rice Kheer ............................................................. 100

Orange Rice Pudding ............................................. 101

Chocolate Brownies ............................................... 102

Gajar Halwa ........................................................... 104

Gulab Jamun .......................................................... 105

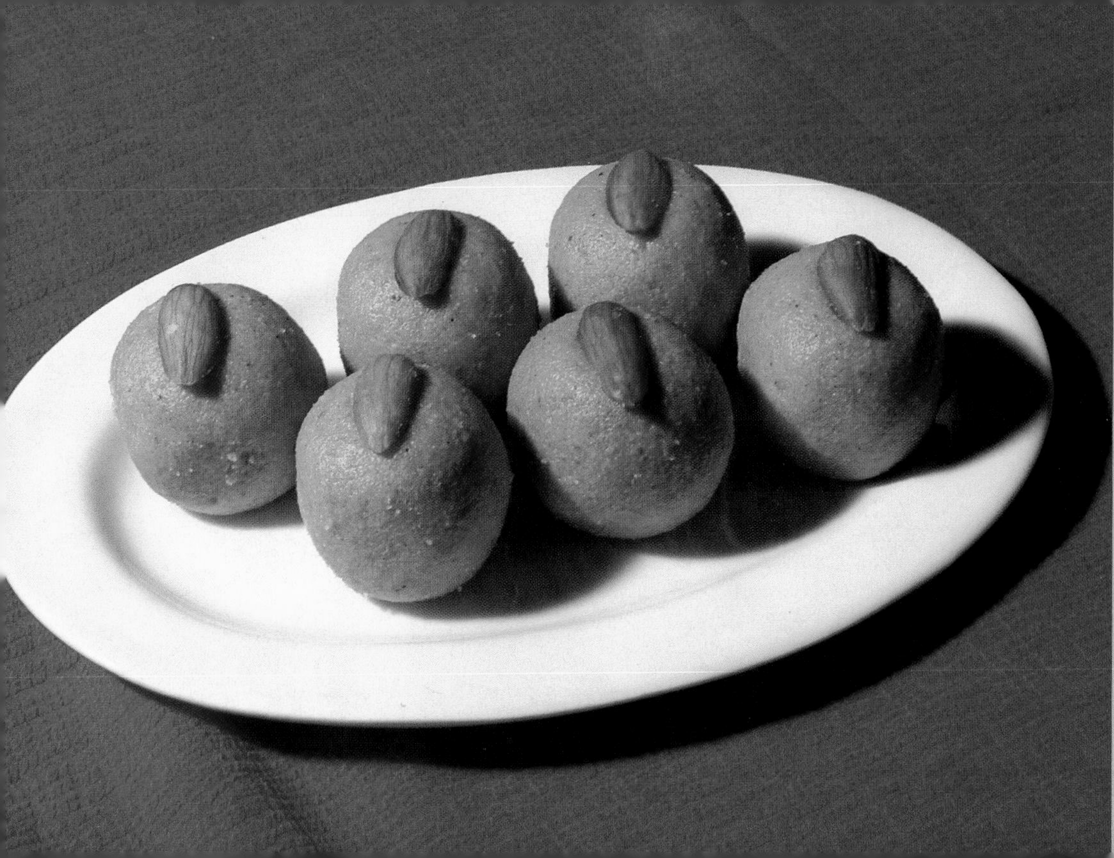

*Badami Besan ke Laddoo*

Boondi aur Bread Pudding

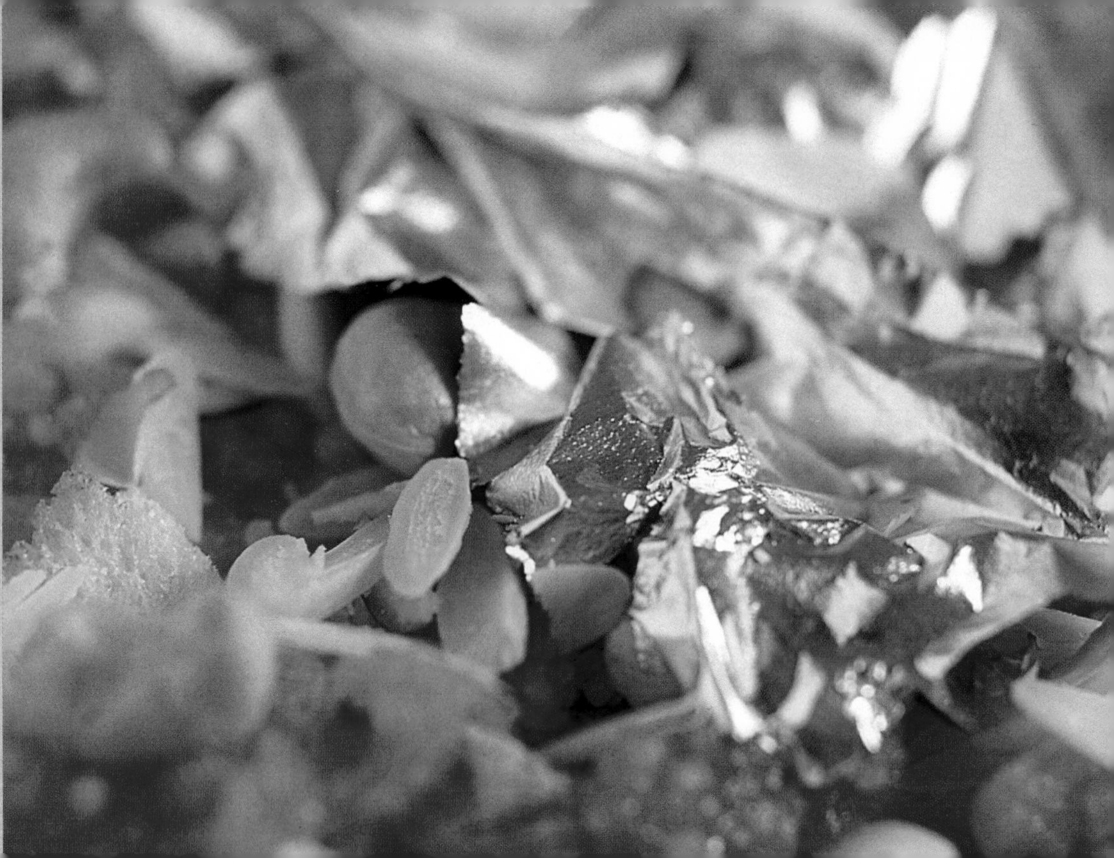

# BOONDI AND BREAD PUDDING

## INGREDIENTS

| | |
|---|---|
| Boondi laddoos ..................... 4 | Cashewnuts ........................... 10 |
| Bread ............................... 6 slices | Rabri ....................... 1½ cups |
| Almonds ................................ 10 | Rose water ........................ 1 tsp |
| Pistachios ............................. 10 | Silver varq ................. 1 sheet |
| Pure ghee .................... 2 tbsps | |

## METHOD OF PREPARATION

1   Blanch, slice almonds and pistachios. Take ghee in a pan and fry cashewnuts till golden brown. Reserve the ghee. Break boondi laddoos to separate into individual boondi.
2   Trim edges of bread slices and cut into triangles.
3   Preheat oven to 220°C.
4   Heat a little ghee on a tawa and toast bread triangles slightly.

5   Spread half of the slices in a baking dish.
6   Spread half of the *boondi* over the bread traingles evenly.
7   Pour half of the *rabri* over the *boondi*.
8   Spread remaining toasted slices followed by remaining *boondi* and *rabri*.
9   Spread fried cashewnuts, almonds and pistachios on top.
10  Bake in the preheated oven at 220°C for ten minutes.
11  When done, sprinkle rose water and spread silver *varq*. Serve hot.

**CHEF'S TIP**

You can also use condensed milk, slightly thinned with a little plain milk instead of *rabri*.

# SANTRA NI BASUNDI

## INGREDIENTS

Milk ..................................... 4 cups

Condensed milk ................. 1 cup

Oranges (sweet) ......................... 4

Green cardamom powder .. ½ tsp

## METHOD OF PREPARATION

1  Boil milk in a saucepan and reduce till thick and creamy. Add condensed milk and boil for another twenty minutes. Remove, cool and keep it in the refrigerator.

2  Peel two oranges and extract the juice. Strain. Of the remaining two oranges, peel, separate into segments, remove pith and seeds and slice. When milk is ice cold, add orange juice, sliced segments and cardamom powder.

3  Serve very cold as a sweet with *puris*.

# BADAMI BESAN KE LADDOO

## INGREDIENTS

Gram flour (*besan*) ........... 4 cups
Almonds ............................. 20-25
*Ghee* ......................... 2 cups

Green cardamom powder ...... ½ tsp
Powdered sugar ................. 2 cups

## METHOD OF PREPARATION

1 Heat *ghee* in a *kadai* and add green cardamom powder.
2 Add gram flour and roast on low heat for approximately ten minutes.
3 Crush almonds.
4 Transfer roasted gram flour to a bowl and add crushed almonds and mix.
5 Allow the mixture to cool slightly before adding powdered sugar.
6 Add sugar and mix. Roll into even sized *laddoos*. Cool and store.

# BLACK CURRANT KULFI WITH MANGO SALSA

## INGREDIENTS

Milk .................................. 10 cups
Black currants .................. ¼ cup
Mangoes (ripe) ........ 2 large sized
Cashewnuts.............................. 10
Condensed milk ............... ¾ cup

Fresh cream ........................½ cup
Lemon juice ......................1 tbsp
Honey ................................1 tbsp
Red chilli flakes ................ ¼ tsp

## METHOD OF PREPARATION

1   Soak black currants in half a cup of warm water for fifteen minutes. Drain and grind coarsely. Grind cashewnuts coarsely.

2   Heat milk in a saucepan and bring it to a boil. Let it boil, stirring continuously, till reduced to three-fourths the original quantity. Add

condensed milk and keep stirring.

3　Add coarsely ground cashewnuts and cook till it thickens.

4　Remove from heat and let it cool completely.

5　In a large bowl take ground black currants and fresh cream and whisk well. Add reduced milk. Mix well.

6　Pour into *kulfi* moulds, seal them airtight and place them in the freezer till set.

7　Wash, peel mangoes and cut the flesh into half inch sized cubes.

8　To serve, arrange mango cubes in a serving plate. Demould the *kulfi* and place it amid the mango cubes.

9　Mix lemon juice, honey and chilli flakes and sprinkle over the mango cubes. Serve immediately.

# KHUBANI KA MEETHA

## INGREDIENTS

Dry apricots *(khubani)* ..... ½ kg
Milk ...................... 5 cups (1 litre)
Saffron ....................... 7-8 strands
Raisins ............................. 2 tbsps

Sugar ................................... ½ cup
*Khoya/mawa* (grated) ...... 3 tbsps
Silver *varq* ............. as required

## METHOD OF PREPARATION

1   Soak dry apricots in sufficient water for half an hour, drain. Boil in four to five cups of water for thirty minutes. When soft, drain and refresh with cold water. Mash into a pulp, discarding the stones.
2   Mix saffron with a tablespoon of warm milk. Wash and soak raisins in a cup of water for ten minutes and drain.
3   Boil milk in a pan till it is reduced to almost half its quantity. Add sugar, crumbled *khoya*, raisins and boil for another five minutes. Add saffron milk and mix well. Remove from heat and let it cool.
4   Mix together apricot pulp and reduced milk.
5   Portion out into individual bowls and serve chilled garnished with silver *varq*.

# CHANAR PAYESH

## INGREDIENTS

| | | | |
|---|---|---|---|
| Milk | 3½ lts | Pistachios | 7-8 |
| Lemon juice | 1½ tbsps | Sugar | 1¼ cups |
| Almonds | 5-6 | Rose water | 1 tsp |

## METHOD OF PREPARTION

1 Boil one and a half litres of milk in a pan. Add lemon juice just when it comes to a boil and let it curdle. Separate the *chenna* (curdled milk) from the whey and let it cool slightly. Then knead it thoroughly.

2 Blanch almonds and pistachios in one cup of boiling water. Drain, peel and chop finely.

3 Bring remaining two litres of milk to a boil, reduce heat and let it simmer till reduced to half.

4 Add sugar and nuts and cook till sugar dissolves.

5 Add *chenna*, mix well and simmer for another ten minutes.

6 Remove from heat and add rose water. Serve at room temperature.

Chanar Payesh

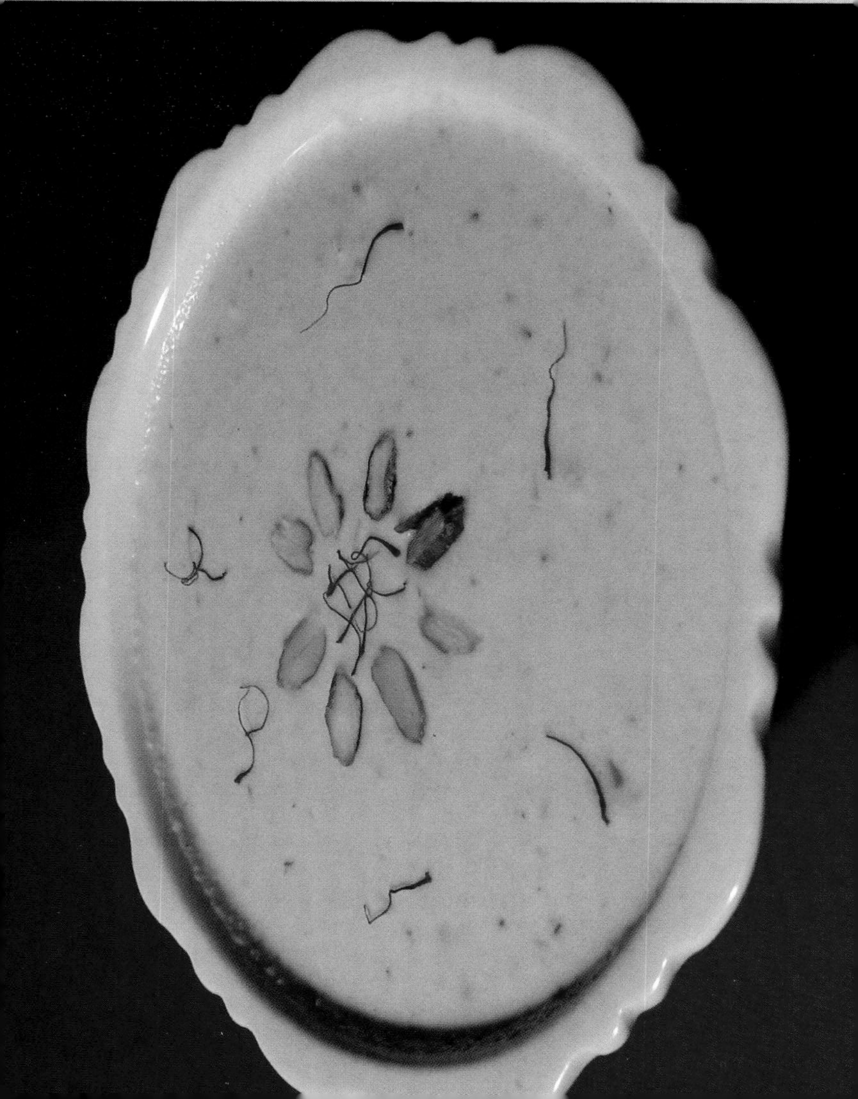

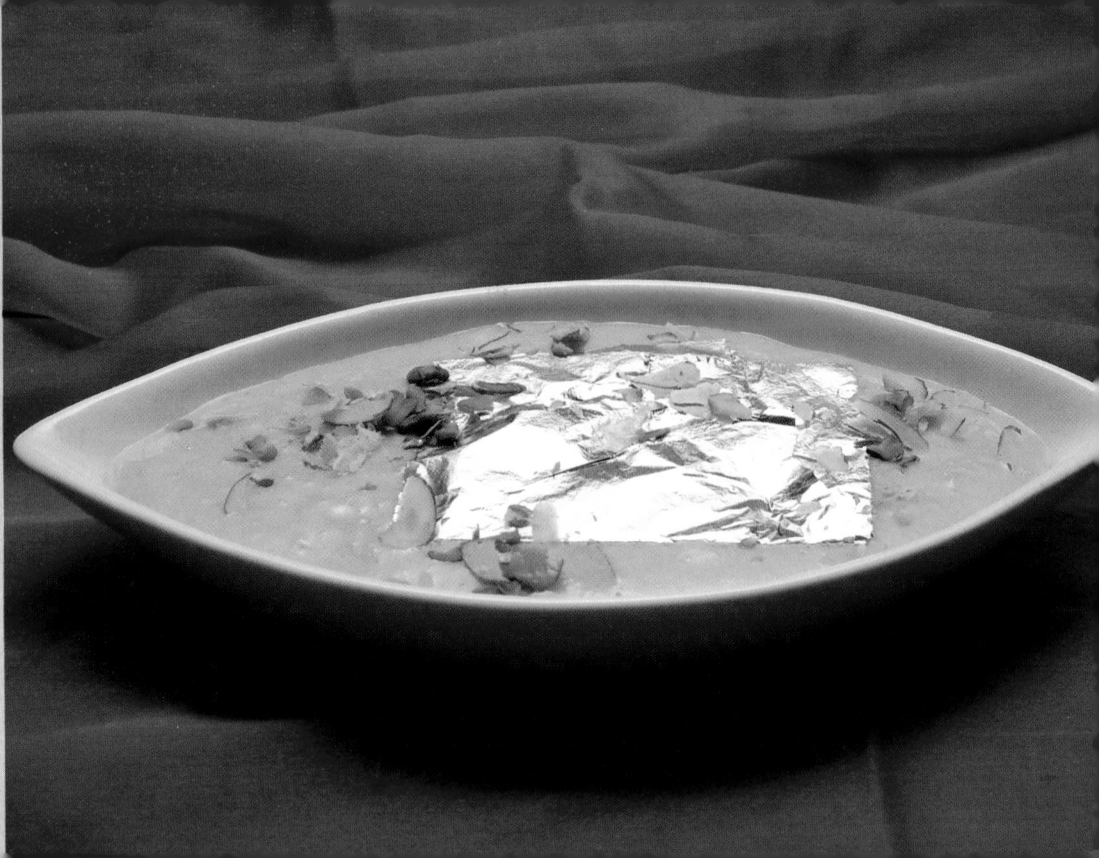

Khubani ka Meetha

Motichoor Laddoo

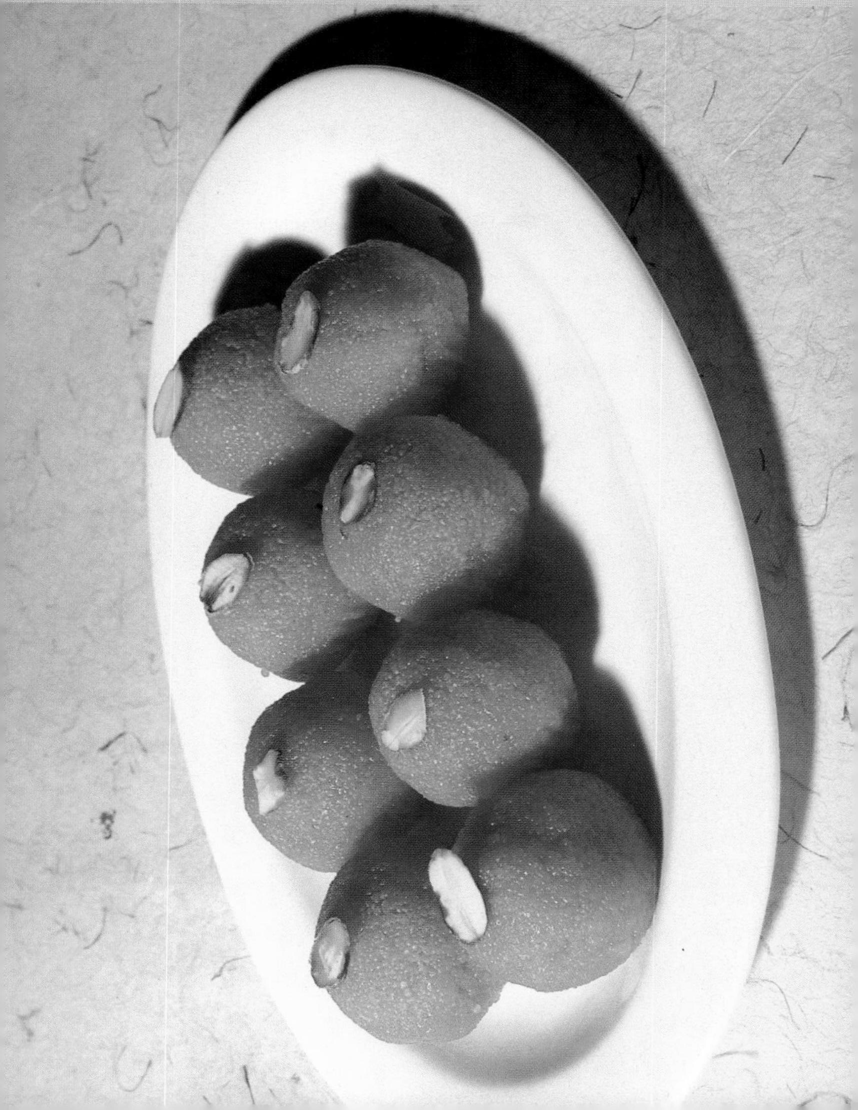

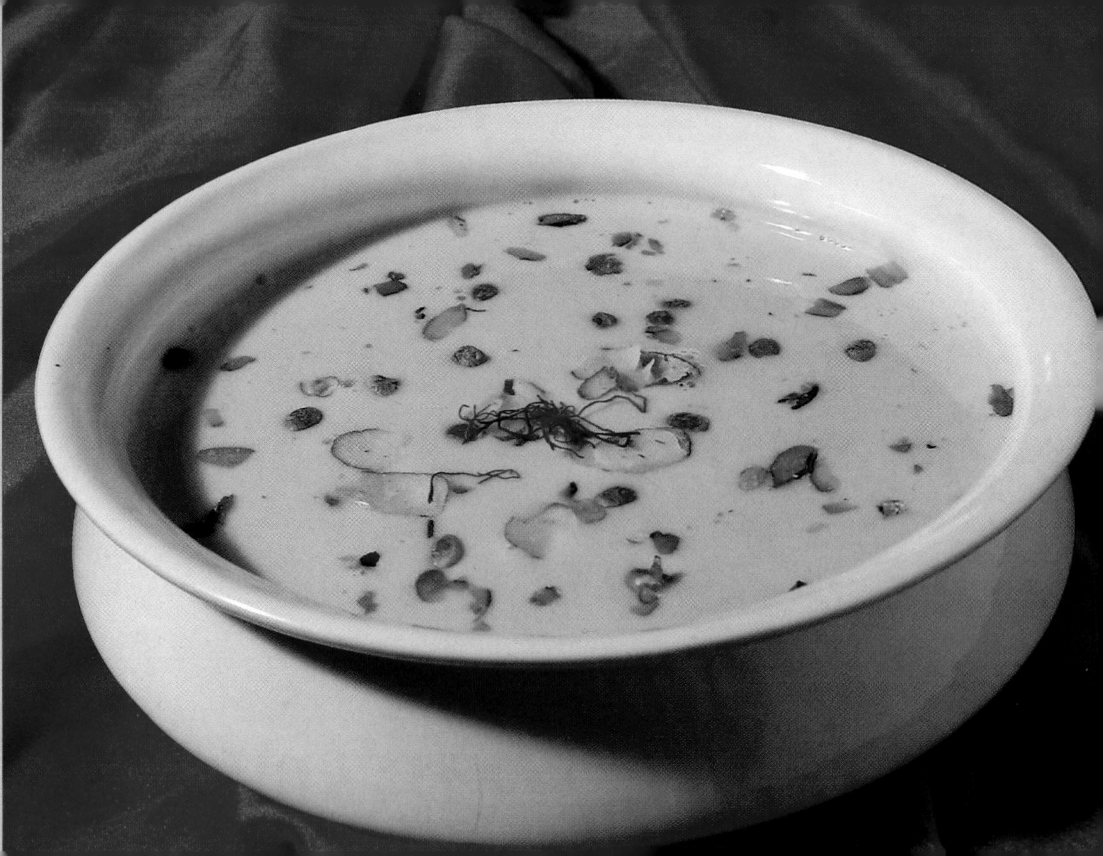

Basoondi

# BASOONDI

## INGREDIENTS

Milk .................................7 ½ cups
Almonds ............................. ½ cup
Sunflower seeds (*chironji*) ..... 2 tbsps

Pistachios ............................. 8-10
Sugar ....................................¾ cup
Saffron ..................... a few strands

## METHOD OF PREPARATION

1 Soak almonds in one cup of warm water to blanch. Remove skin. Reserve a few for garnishing and make a paste of the rest.
2 Slice reserved almonds and pistachios. Wash and pat dry *chironji*.
3 Bring milk to a boil, stirring continuously. Simmer over low heat till milk coats the back of the spoon.
4 Stir in almond paste dissolved in half a cup of water or milk and mix well. Add sugar and saffron and cook till sugar gets fully dissolved.
5 Chill and serve garnished with sliced almonds, pistachios and *chironji*.

# MOTICHOOR LADDOO

## INGREDIENTS

| | | | |
|---|---|---|---|
| Gram flour (*besan*) | 2½ cups | Pistachios | 10 |
| Sugar | 1¾ cups | Lemon yellow or orange colo ... ras required |
| Milk | ¼ cup | *Ghee* | to deep fry |
| Almonds | 10 | Green cardamom seeds | 1 tbsp |

## METHOD OF PREPARATION

1 Cook sugar with three cups of water to make syrup of one thread consistency. Add milk and when the scum rises to the top, remove it. Add colour as desired and keep the syrup aside. Blanch almonds and pistachios in one cup of hot water for five minutes. Drain, peel and cut into slivers. Make a thin batter of *besan* with three cups of water (pouring consistency). Add colour as desired.

2 Heat sufficient *ghee* in a *kadai*. Hold a perforated spoon over the hot *ghee*, pour a little batter over it and pass the batter through it fast into the *kadai* to make *boondis*. Fry for about two to three minutes. Remove the *boondis* using a slotted spoon, drain thoroughly and put into the syrup.

3 When the *boondis* have absorbed all the syrup add cardamom seeds and mix gently. Divide into twenty-five portions and shape each into a *laddoo*. Garnish with slivers of pistachios or almonds. Cool and store. These *laddoos* do not stay for long and therefore should be consumed fast.

# CHANDRAKALA

## INGREDIENTS

Refined flour (*maida*) ........ 1 cup
Salt ................................... a pinch
Ghee ...... 1½ tbsps + to deep fry
**For the filling** ...............................
*Khoya/mawa*(grated) ........ ¾ cup

Castor sugar ....................... ½ cup
Green cardamom powder .. ½ tsp
**For the syrup**
Sugar ............................... 1¼ cups
Saffron ..................... a few strands

## METHOD OF PREPARATION

1  Sieve flour and salt together. Rub in *ghee* and knead into a firm dough using water as required. Cover and keep aside.

2  Place *khoya* in a thick-bottomed pan. Cook on low heat for three to four minutes. Add castor sugar and green cardamom powder and remove from heat. Let it cool.

3  Cook sugar with five cups of water to make a sugar syrup of one-thread consistency. Add saffron to it. Keep it aside.

4  Divide dough into twenty equal parts. Roll out two parts into *puris*.

Place one tablespoon of *khoya* filling in the centre on one *puri* and cover with the other *puri*. Wet the edges and seal firmly. Prepare more *chandrakalas* in the same way.

5 Heat sufficient *ghee* in a *kadai* and deep-fry *chandrakalas* on medium heat till golden brown. Drain away excess *ghee* and soak immediately in hot syrup.

6 When it is coated on all sides with sugar syrup, gently remove and serve.

# ZAFRANI PULAO

## INGREDIENTS

Basmati rice ........................ 2 cups
Ghee .......................... 4 tbsps
Raisins ............................... 25-30
Almonds ............................... 20
Cashewnuts............................ 12

Nutmeg powder ................. ¼ tsp
Green cardamom powder.. ½ tsp
Milk ....................................... ½ cup
Sugar ...................................½ cup
Saffron ............................. a pinch

## METHOD OF PREPARATION

1   Wash rice twice and soak in just enough water to cover it for half
    an hour. Drain. Wash and pat dry raisins.
2   Heat *ghee* in a deep pan and gently fry almonds, cashewnuts and
    raisins. Drain and keep aside. When cool, slice almonds thinly and
    halve cashewnuts. In the same pan add rice and sauté gently for two to
    three minutes. Add nutmeg powder and green cardamom powder.
3   Boil milk and sugar adding saffron. Add to rice with three and a
    half cups of water. Add raisins. Stir once.
4   Cover and cook on low heat till done. Allow standing time of five minutes.
5   Garnish with almonds and cashewnuts. Serve hot.

# KALAKAND

## INGREDIENTS

| | | | |
|---|---|---|---|
| Milk | 10 cups | **For garnish** | |
| Alum (*phitkari*) | ¼ tsp | Pistachios | 15-20 |
| Sugar | ¾ cup | Silver *varq* | as required |
| Ghee | 1 tbsp | | |

## METHOD OF PREPARATION

1 Slice pistachios thinly for garnish.
2 Boil milk till it thickens a little. Crush alum and add to thickened milk. Keep stirring till milk becomes granular. Keep on cooking till most of the moisture evaporates and it remains a solid mass.
3 Add sugar and mix well. Cook further for five to ten minutes till it thickens again. Take an aluminium tray and grease it with a little *ghee*. Pour milk mixture into the tray and level. Garnish with pistachios. Allow it to set for a few hours in a cool and dry place.
4 When properly set, decorate with silver *varq* and cut into squares or diamond shaped pieces and serve.

Note: *Kalakand* does not keep for long so it should be used up immediately.

# DUDHI HALWA

## INGREDIENTS

Bottle gourd (*dudhi/lauki*) ..........
.............. 1 medium sized (½ kg)
Milk ...................................3 cups
Cashewnuts............................ 10
Pistachios ................................. 10

Raisins .......................................10
Pure *ghee* .................3-4 tbsps
Sugar ....................................¼ cup
Green cardamom powder ... ½ tsp

## METHOD OF PREPARATION

1  Wash, peel gourd and scrape out seeds.  Grate it finely.
2  Chop cashewnuts and pistachios roughly. Wash and pat dry raisins.
3  Heat milk in a saucepan and reduce to around two cups.
4  Heat *ghee* in a pan, add grated gourd and sauté for five to seven minutes.
5  Add reduced milk and cook, stirring continuously, till the liquid
   content has evaporated. Add sugar and green cardamom powder.
   Mix thoroughly.
6  Serve hot or cold garnished with cashewnuts, raisins and pistachios.

# STRAWBERRY
# CHEESE CAKE

## INGREDIENTS

**Crust**
Bran biscuits or Digestive biscuits
.................................................. 8-10
Margarine ........................... 1 tbsp
Instant coffee powder ......... 1 tsp
**Filling**
Fresh strawberries ..... 12 medium sized
Skimmed milk cottage cheese ....... 1½ cups
Skimmed milk yogurt .... 1½ cups
Sugar (powdered) ............. ½ cup

Carregnan ........................... 1 tbsp
Skimmed milk ................... 1 cup
Cornstarch ......................... 1 tbsp
Lemon rind ............ of one lemon
Vanilla essence ..................... 1 tsp
Strawberry essence .............. 1 tsp
**Topping**
Fresh strawberries .... 6-8 medium sized
Strawberry or lemon-jelly ..... 1 tbsp

## METHOD OF PREPARATION

1   Crush biscuits to a coarse powder. Melt margarine in a pan. Boil two teaspoons of water in a separate bowl and dissolve instant coffee powder and cool slightly.

2   Combine melted margarine and dissolved coffee with the crushed biscuits. Line a six inch spring form pan with butter paper. Press mixture evenly over bottom of the prepared pan. Set aside.

3   Soak carregnan in a quarter cup of water. Heat it lightly on a double boiler to dissolve and keep warm. Wash, hull strawberries and roughly chop. For the topping, slice strawberries and keep aside.

4   Dissolve cornstarch in two tablespoons of milk. Heat rest of the milk in a pan. Add blended cornstarch to it. Cook on low heat till it thickens. Remove from heat and cool it to room temperature.

5   Hang yogurt in a muslin cloth for about half an hour. Place cottage cheese and hung yogurt in a food processor or blender and process until smooth. Add remaining ingredients for the filling. Process just until blended, scraping sides of bowl frequently.

6   Pour filling into the prepared pan. Cover and chill for at least two hours or until set.

7   Dissolve strawberry or lemon jelly in a quarter cup of water, bring it to a boil and cool.

8   Decorate the top of the chilled cheesecake with sliced strawberries and brush liberally with the prepared jelly. Chill until the jelly is set.

9   Remove from the spring form pan and cut into eight wedges with a sharp knife dipped in hot water.

# LAVANG LATIKA

## INGREDIENTS

*Khoya/mawa* (grated) ....... ¾ cup
*Ghee* ........ 3 tbsps + to deep fry
Almonds ..................................... 6
Pistachios ................................... 8
Green cardamoms ..................... 4
Icing sugar .......................... 1 tbsp
Clove powder ..................... ¼ tsp

Refined flour (*maida*) ....... 2 cups
Soda bicarbonate ............ a pinch
Cloves ..................................... 12
Silver *varq* ............. as required
**For syrup**
Sugar ..................................... 3 cups

## METHOD OF PREPARATION

1   Sauté *khoya* with one tablespoon of *ghee* for two to three minutes, remove and cool.
2   Blanch almonds and pistachios in half a cup of hot water for five minutes. Drain, peel and cut into slivers.
3   Crush cardamoms coarsely. Add icing sugar, slivered almonds, pistachios, clove powder to the *khoya* mixture and mix well. Keep aside.

4   Sieve together flour and soda bicarbonate. Rub in two tablespoons of *ghee* till the mixture resembles breadcrumbs.

5   Knead into a firm dough using water as required. Rest the dough for about twenty minutes. Divide dough into twelve equal portions, shape into balls and roll out into three to four inch diameter discs. Apply little *ghee* on the discs and dust with little flour.

6   Now place one tablespoon of *khoya* mixture in the centre of each disc, apply little water on edges and fold to form a square. Seal firmly. Press in a clove on each *latika* for holding it together as also for garnish.

7   Mix sugar with two cups of water and cook to form a syrup of two-thread consistency.

8   Heat sufficient *ghee* in a *kadai* and deep-fry three to four *latikas* at a time on medium heat till lightly browned. Drain and soak in sugar syrup for fifteen to twenty minutes.

9   Remove squares with a slotted spoon onto a tray and let them dry.

10  Serve garnished with silver *varq*.

# SCOOPY FRUIT CARAMEL

## INGREDIENTS

Mangoes (ripe) .... 2 medium sized
Watermelon ...... ¼ medium sized
Muskmelon ....... ½ medium sized
Papaya .............. ½ medium sized
Almonds .............................. 8-10
Sugar ................................. 1 tbsp
Honey ............................... 1 tbsp

Fruit juice ........................... 1 cup
*Gulkand* ..................... 2 tbsps
Vanilla ice-cream .......... 4 scoops
Strawberry sauce ............. 6 tbsps
Butterscotch ice-cream 4 scoops
Chocolate sauce ............. 6 tbsps
Wafer biscuits ...................... 4-8

## METHOD OF PREPARATION

1   Wash, cut mangoes and remove seeds. Wash, cut watermelon, muskmelon and papaya. Scoop out fruits (discarding the seeds) with a Parisienne scoop and place in a glass bowl.

2   Blanch almonds in one cup of warm water. Drain, peel and cut into slivers.

3   Combine sugar and honey in a pan. Place on low heat and cook, stirring continuously, till sugar melts and gets completely blended with honey. Remove from heat.

4   Add half a cup of water and fruit juice to the honey-sugar blend. Stir in *gulkand*.

5   Add this to the fruit scoops and place bowl in the refrigerator to chill.

6   To serve, take a beer mug or a glass bowl. Make a layer of fruit scoops, place a scoop of vanilla ice-cream topped with almond slivers, dribble some strawberry sauce. Top this with a second layer of fruit scoops, covered with a scoop of butterscotch ice-cream and top it up with chocolate sauce. Garnish with almond slivers and wafer biscuits. Decorate with a small paper umbrella and serve immediately.

# CHOCOLATE WALNUT BURFI

## INGREDIENTS

*Khoya/mawa* (grated) ...2 ½ cups
Walnut kernels .................. ½ cup
Sugar .................................... ½ cup

Milk .................................... 3 tbsps
Dark chocolate ............. 1 ½ cups
Oil ............................. for greasing

## METHOD OF PREPARATION

1. Roughly chop walnuts, keeping a few aside for garnish.
2. Heat a pan, add *khoya* and roast for four to five minutes.
3. Add sugar, chopped walnuts and milk and cook till it thickens.
4. Melt dark chocolate in a double boiler. Pass it through a sieve to remove any lumps. Bring melted chocolate to room temperature.
5. Divide the cooked *khoya* mixture into three equal parts. To one part add one-third of melted chocolate. Mix well.
6. Grease a tray with oil. Pour one part of plain *khoya* mixture onto it

and spread evenly. Shake the tray so that mixture spreads evenly. Now spread the chocolate *khoya* mixture over and finally top with remaining plain *khoya* mixture. Let it cool for forty-five minutes to one hour. When completely cooled, cut into square or diamond shaped pieces and keep.

7   Holding the *burfi* pieces by their edges dip into the remaining melted chocolate so that only the topside of the *burfi* is covered with chocolate. Garnish with walnut pieces and keep it in refrigerator for thirty minutes before serving.

**Note:** A double boiler contains of two pots, one which sits on top of the other. The bottom pot contains boiling water, the top pot contains whatever is being cooked. This tool is useful for making delicate sauces or melting chocolate or any other occasion when you don't want to have direct heat on the food, which is being cooked. You can improvise a double boiler by placing the items to be cooked in a metal bowl, which is placed over a pot of boiling water.

# KAJU KATLI

## INGREDIENTS

Cashewnut powder ....... 3 ½ cups

Sugar .......................... 1 1/3 cups

Water .......................... 1 1/3 cups

Liquid glucose ................. 2 tbsps

Ghee ...................... 1 ½ tbsps

Silver *varq* ............. as required

## METHOD OF PREPARATION

1 Cook sugar and water together till the syrup reaches 118°C and you get multi strings. Then add liquid glucose and *ghee* and stir well.

2 Remove from heat and add cashewnut powder stirring continuously. If necessary add one tablespoon of water and keep stirring till the temperature comes down to 65°C.

3 Knead lightly to make a soft dough. Roll out on a flat greased surface to one centimetre thickness.

4 Rub a butter paper over the surface to smoothen it evenly. Apply silver *varq* and cut into diamond shapes. Store in an airtight container.

*Kaju Katli Chocolate Walnut Burfi*

Ukdiche Modak/ Rava Naral Laddoo

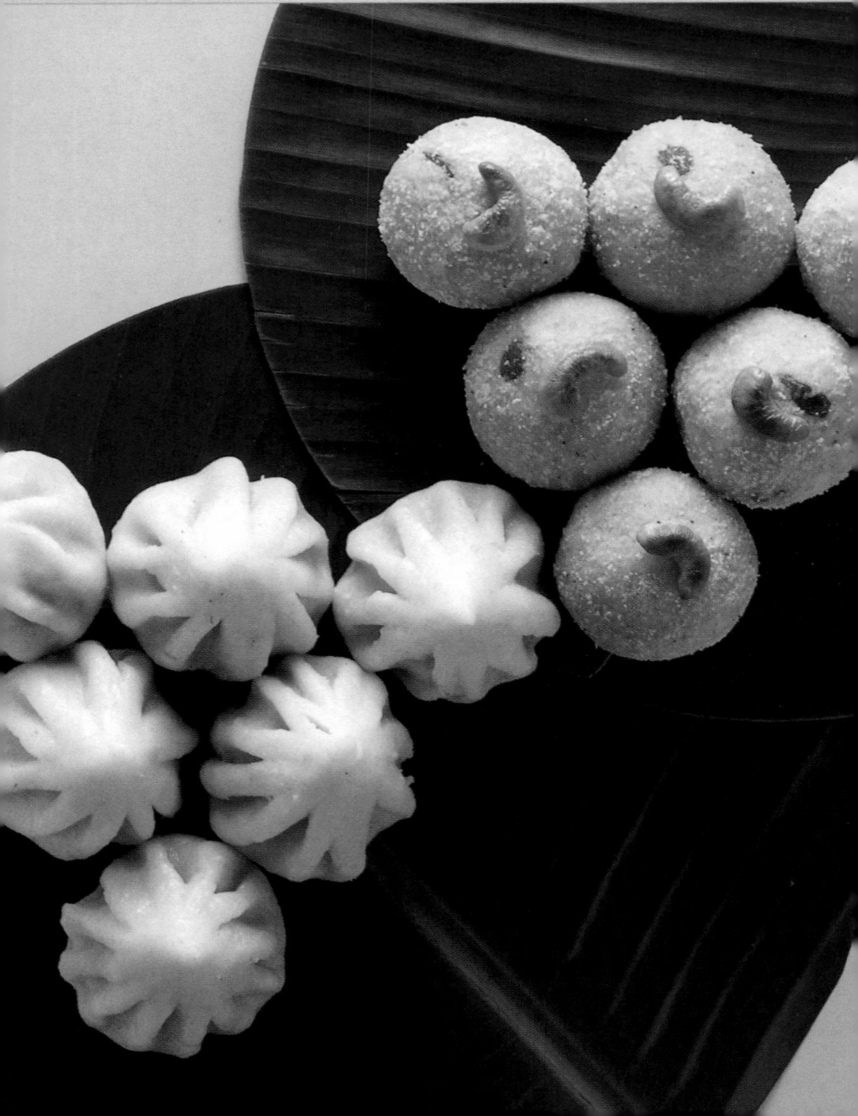

# UKDICHE MODAK

## INGREDIENTS

Rice ..................................... 2 cups
Pure *ghee* ...................... 1 tbsp
Salt .................................... a pinch

**For stuffing**
Coconut (scraped) ........ 1½ cups
Jaggery (grated) ................. ¾ cup
Green cardamom powder ... ½ tsp

## METHOD OF PREPARATION

1  Clean, wash and drain rice thoroughly. Dry completely by spreading on an absorbent sheet of cloth. Grind to a fine powder. Pass it through a fine sieve.

2  Bring one and a quarter cups of water to boil in a pan, add salt and *ghee* to it.

3  Add rice flour in a flow, stirring continuously to prevent lumps from forming. Remove the pan from heat and keep it covered for ten to fifteen minutes.

4  Grease your palms with a little oil and knead the cooked rice

mixture to a soft dough. Keep covered with a moist cloth.

5  Combine coconut with jaggery in a pan and cook on medium heat for one or two minutes or till light golden brown. Ensure that it is not overcooked. Add green cardamom powder and remove from heat and cool it slightly. Divide coconut mixture into ten to twelve equal portions.

6  Divide dough into ten to twelve lemon sized balls. With greased palms flatten each ball to form discs of three inches diameter. Press edges of the discs further to reduce the thickness.

7  Place a portion of coconut-jaggery mixture in the centre, form eight to ten pleats with fingers, gather them together to form a bundle and seal the edges at the top.

8  Steam them in an *idli* steamer for ten to twelve minutes. Serve hot *modak* with pure *ghee*.

# RAWA NARAL LADDOO

## INGREDIENTS

Semolina (*rawa*)............1½ cups
Coconut (scraped) ........... ¾ cup
Pure *ghee* ..................... 4 tbsps

Raisins ............................... 2 tbsps
Sugar .................................... 1 cup
Green cardamom powder ... ½ tsp

## METHOD OF PREPARATION

1  Heat *ghee* in a thick-bottomed *kadai*, stir-fry semolina on low heat till it just starts changing colour to light golden. Add coconut. Continue to stir-fry for one more minute. Wash raisins and pat them dry.

2  Cook sugar with half a cup of water on medium heat, stirring continuously till it dissolves. Increase heat and bring the syrup to a boil. Cook without stirring for about five minutes or till it reaches single thread consistency.

3  Add warm roasted semolina mixture and green cardamom powder to sugar syrup and mix well. Cover with a lid and keep aside for thirty minutes, stirring the mixture at regular intervals.

4  Divide mixture into twelve to fifteen equal portions. Shape into firm *laddoos* and decorate with raisins.

# FRUIT KABABS WITH BLACK CURRANT DIP

## INGREDIENTS

Peaches .......................................... 5
Plums ............................................. 5
Apple ....................... 1 large sized
Pineapple ........................... 2 slices
Bananas .................... 2 large sized
Kiwi fruit .................. 1 large sized
**For basting**
Brown sugar ...................... 3 tbsps
Honey ................................. ¼ cup
Lemon juice ...................... 3 tbsps

Salt .................................... to taste
Fresh mint leaves ...... a few sprigs
Oil .................................... 2 tbsps
**For black currant dip**
Black currants ................... 20-25
Sugar .................................. 3 tbsps
Lemon juice ...................... 2 tbsps
Salt .................................... to taste
Red chilli flakes .................. 1 tsp
Chilli sauce .......................... 1 tbsp

## METHOD OF PREPARATION

1  Wash and cut peaches, plums, apple, pineapple slices into one and a half inch sized pieces. Peel and cut bananas and kiwi into one and a half inch sized pieces. Clean, wash and chop mint leaves.

2  Soak the wooden skewers in water for half an hour. Skewer the fruits in this order: apple, peach, kiwi, pineapple, plum, banana and apple. Use up all the pieces similarly.

3  For the dip, soak black currants in a cup of hot water for fifteen minutes. Drain and puree them in a mixer.

4  Heat puree in a pan along with one-fourth cup of water, sugar, lemon juice and cook stirring continuously.

5  Heat a griddle and grease it. Place the skewers and grill.

6  Mix brown sugar, honey, lemon juice, salt and chopped mint leaves. Add oil and mix. Pour a little of this mixture over the fruits as they are cooking. Keep rotating the skewers so that the fruits get cooked from all sides. Pour the remaining honey mixture.

7  Add salt, red chilli flakes to the black currant sauce and mix. Add chilli sauce and mix.

8  Place the skewers on a serving plate and pour the black currant sauce over and serve hot.

# DATE ROLLS

## INGREDIENTS

| | | | |
|---|---|---|---|
| Dates (seedless) | 2 cups | Cashewnuts | 10-15 |
| Poppy seeds | 3 tbsps | Pistachios | 10-15 |
| Almonds | 10-15 | *Ghee* | 4 tbsps |

## METHOD OF PREPARATION

1 Chop dates and keep aside. Dry roast poppy seeds and keep aside. Grind almonds, cashewnuts and pistachios to a coarse powder.

2 Heat *ghee* in a *kadai*, add chopped dates and cover and cook on low heat for five to six minutes. Add ground almonds, cashewnuts and pistachios and cook further on low heat for four to five minutes till the mixture is soft and well blended.

3 Remove from heat, spread evenly to one centimetre thickness on a greased *thali* and allow to cool.

4 When cool cut into strips, fold tightly to form rolls, coat with poppy seeds and serve.

# MOONG DAL HALWA

## INGREDIENTS

| | |
|---|---|
| Green gram split (*dhuli moong dal*) ............................................. 1 cup | Milk ...................................... ½ cup |
| | Almonds .............................. 10-12 |
| Sugar ...................................... 1 cup | *Ghee* ........................................... 1 cup |
| Saffron .............. a generous pinch | *Khoya/mawa* (grated) ........ ¾ cup |

## METHOD OF PREPARATION

**CHEF'S TIP**

Add one tablespoon of *besan* to melted ghee before putting the ground *moong dal*. It helps in even cooking of ground *moong dal* and also prevents formation of lumps during cooking.

1 Wash and soak *moong dal* in two cups of water for six hours. Grind it coarsely using very little water.
2 Prepare one-string sugar syrup with sugar and one and half cups of water.
3 Soak saffron in hot milk. Blanch almonds in one cup of boiling hot water for five minutes. Drain, cool, peel and cut into thin slivers.
4 Heat *ghee* in a thick-bottomed pan and add ground *moong dal*. Keep stirring over low heat till *dal* turns golden brown.
5 Add sugar syrup and saffron milk. Stir till they are thoroughly incorporated and *halwa* is of dropping consistency. Add *khoya* and cook till it blends thoroughly.
6 Serve hot garnished with almond slivers.

Moong Dal Halwa

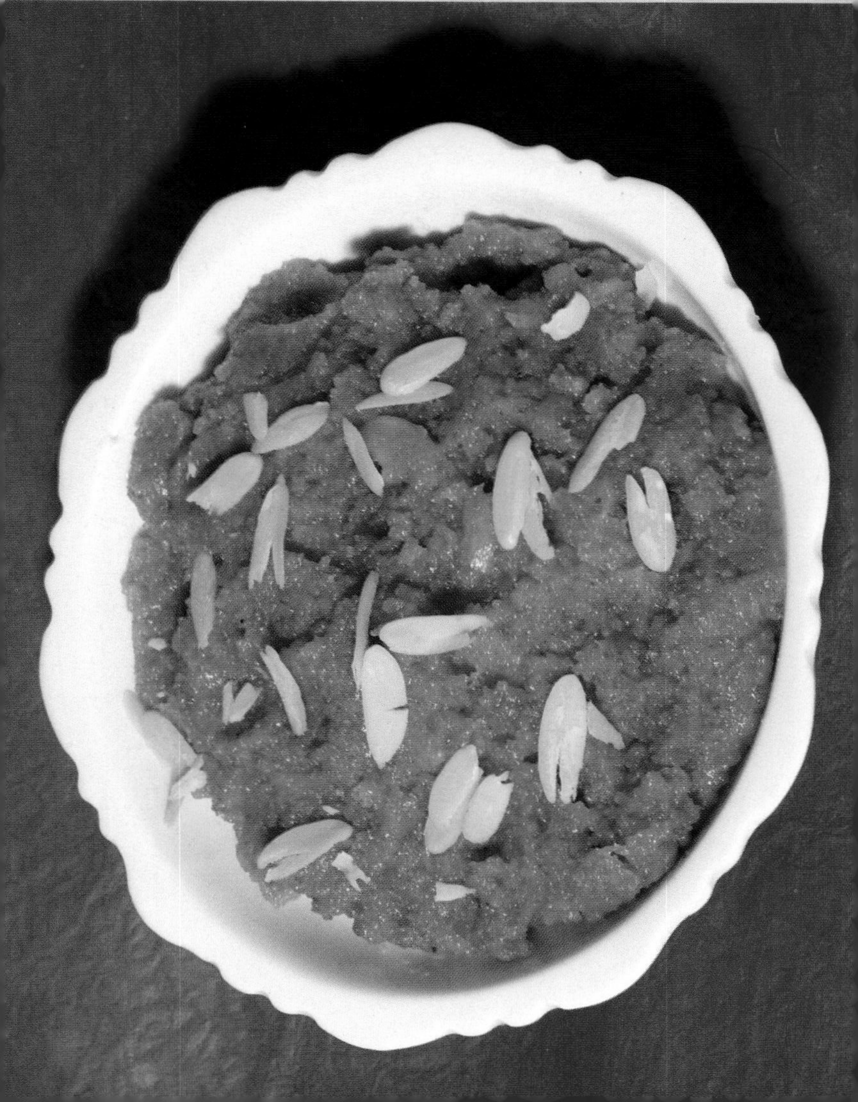

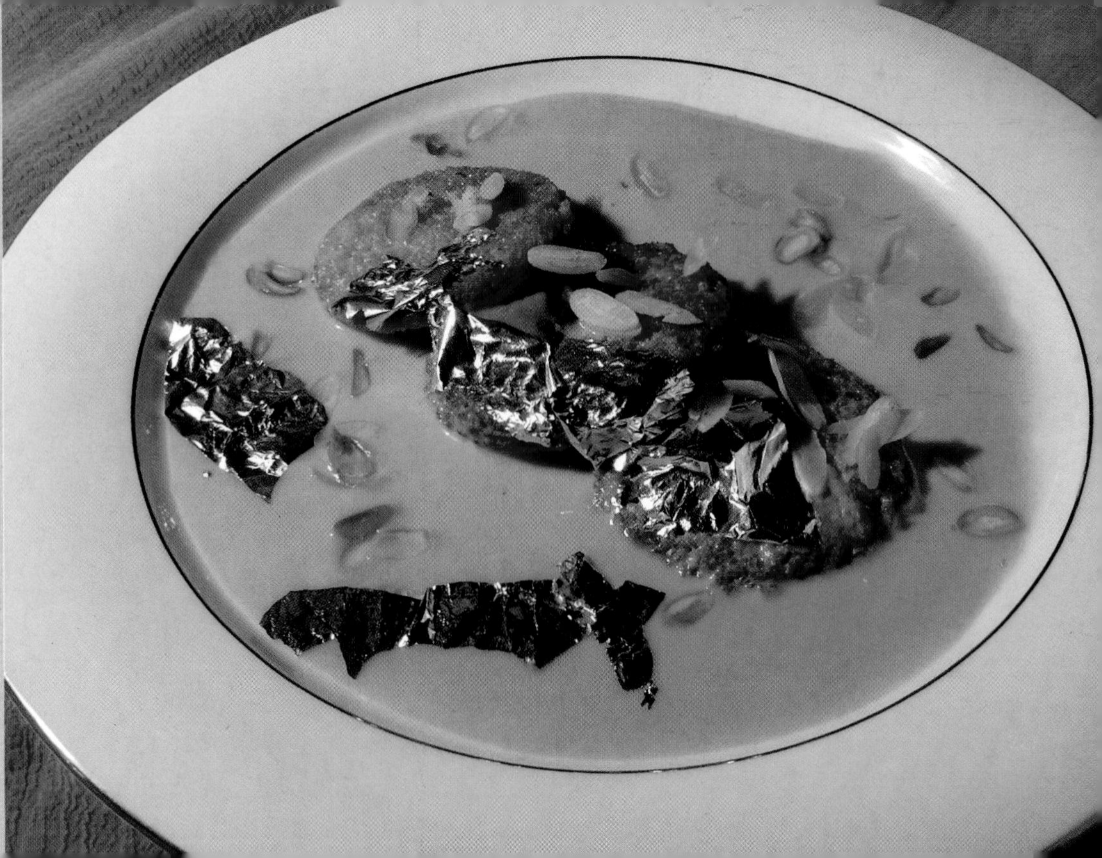

*Khajoori Shahi Tukde*

# KHAJOORI SHAHI TUKRA

## INGREDIENTS

Dates (seedless) .................. 1 cup
Bread ............................... 8 slices
Pure *ghee* ........... to shallow fry
Pistachios .......................... 10-12
Almonds ............................. 8-10

Green cardamom powder .. ½ tsp
Milk ..................................... 5 cups
Sugar ...................................... ½ cup
Silver *varq* .............. for garnish
Rose water .......................... ½ tsp

## METHOD OF PREPARATION

1  Trim crust and cut each bread slice into a round shape with a cookie cutter or a *katori*. Heat two to three tablespoons of pure *ghee* in a pan and shallow fry the bread pieces for about a minute, turn over and fry about a minute more or until light brown and crisp. Drain and remove onto an absorbent kitchen towel or paper.

2  Soak pistachios and almonds in one cup of hot water for ten minutes.

Drain, peel and slice. Reserve one tablespoon of sliced pistachios and almonds for garnish.

3   Finely chop seedless dates, add green cardamom powder and mash thoroughly with a rolling pin. Add pistachios and almonds and mix well. Divide this mixture into four equal portions.

4   Place a portion of date mixture on a piece of fried bread, cover with another piece of fried bread and press to secure.

5   Pour milk in a pan and bring to a boil. Reduce heat and simmer for ten minutes, stirring continuously or until the quantity is reduced to half. Add sugar and continue to simmer for five minutes, stirring continuously.

6   Dip stuffed bread pieces in this mixture for half a minute, remove and keep aside. Cook remaining milk for five to six minutes, stirring continuously or until it thickens to a coating consistency. Remove from heat and chill.

7   Place soaked bread pieces on a serving dish, pour chilled reduced milk on top, apply silver *varq* and top with reserved pistachios and almonds. Serve sprinkled with rose water.

# ADA PRADHAMAN

## INGREDIENTS

| | | | |
|---|---|---|---|
| Ada | 1 cup | Raisins | 2 tbsps |
| Pure *ghee* | ¼ cup | Cashewnuts | 12 |
| Green cardamoms | 4 | Coconut (scraped) | 1½ cups |
| Sugar | 1 tbsp | Palm jaggery | 1 cup |

## METHOD OF PREPARATION

1 Heat two tablespoons of *ghee* in a pan and fry the *ada* lightly.
2 Grind cardamoms with sugar to a fine powder, sieve and keep aside.
3 Wash raisins and pat them dry. Heat two tablespoons of *ghee* and fry the cashewnuts and raisins till light brown.
4 Soak scraped coconut in one cup of warm water, grind and extract thick milk. Repeat the process and make a second extract and keep aside. Break jaggery into smaller pieces.
5 Cook fried *ada* in one cup of boiling water and the second extract of coconut milk till it is soft but holds its shape.

6  Add jaggery and continue cooking till it thickens. Heat remaining *ghee* and add to cooked *ada*.

7  Add first extract of coconut milk. Stir and mix fried cashewnuts and raisins. Stir well and heat through without boiling the mixture.

8  Sprinkle cardamom powder and serve at room temperature.

### Method of preparing Ada

Soak three-fourth cup of raw rice for about an hour in sufficient water, wash and drain well. Dry the soaked rice on a sheet of dry, absorbent cloth for twenty minutes and grind to a fine powder. Sieve and mix with one cup of warm water to make a thick paste. Spread this batter on a piece of banana leaf, roll and tie with a string. Steam the rolls for fifteen minutes on high heat and cool. Peel the *ada* from the leaves and cut into small discs. Dry overnight and use. If you want to store them for future use then dry well under hot sun and keep in an airtight container.

CHEF'S TIP

Normally readymade *ada* is available at any shop specializing in South Indian items. *Ada* can also be made at home.

# GUR AUR BADAM KI PHIRNI

## INGREDIENTS

Skimmed milk ..................... 3 cups
Rice ...................................... ¼ cup
Almonds .............................. 8-10
Jaggery (grated) .............. 4 tbsps

Pistachios ................................ 4-6
Green cardamom powder.. ½ tsp
Rose water ............................ 1 tsp

## METHOD OF PREPARATION

1  Soak pistachios and almonds in hot water for five minutes. Drain, peel and cut pistachios into slivers. Crush almonds into small bits.
2  Pick, wash and soak rice in sufficient water for thirty minutes. Drain and grind the soaked rice into a fairly smooth paste. Dilute the rice paste in half a cup of water and keep aside.
3  Boil milk in a non-stick saucepan, reduce heat, and add ground rice mixture. Cook on medium heat for about five minutes, stirring

continuously or till the mixture thickens.

4   Add jaggery, crushed almonds and cardamom powder. Reduce heat and cook till jaggery has completely dissolved. (You may notice a little curdling of milk. Ignore, as it is quite common for some varieties of jaggery to have this effect on milk.) Remove from heat and stir in rose water.

5   Remove and pour into separate serving bowls, preferably earthenware. Garnish with pistachios.

6   Chill it in the refrigerator for an hour before serving.

# CHOCO COCONUT LADDOO

## INGREDIENTS

| | | | |
|---|---|---|---|
| Chocolate | 2 cups | Walnuts | 8-10 |
| Condensed milk | 1 cup | Almonds | 8-10 |
| Desiccated coconut | 2½ cups | Pistachios | 8-10 |

## METHOD OF PREPARATION

1  Crush walnuts and coarsely grind almonds. Blanch pistachios in half a cup of hot water for five minutes. Drain and peel.
2  Grate chocolate and melt it in a double boiler. Stir and continue to heat it for another half a minute. Remove and blend in condensed milk. Mix in one and half cups of desiccated coconut, walnuts and almonds.
3  Shape into round *laddoos*. Roll in the remaining desiccated coconut and garnish with blanched whole pistachio on each *laddoo*.

# GIL-E-FIRDAUS

## INGREDIENTS

| | | | |
|---|---|---|---|
| Rice | ¼ cup | Milk | 10 cups |
| Red pumpkin | 250 gms | *Khoya/mawa* (grated) | ½ cup |
| Almonds | 10 | Sugar | ½ cup |
| Pineapple slices | 2 | Rose essence | a few drops |
| Rose petals | a few petals | Glace cherries | 4-5 |
| Ghee | 2 tbsps | | |

## METHOD OF PREPARATION

1   Pick, wash and soak rice for thirty minutes to one hour in one cup of water. Drain and keep aside. Peel, wash and grate pumpkin. Boil three cups of water and add pumpkin. Cook till soft, drain and keep aside.

2   Soak almonds in hot water for five minutes. Drain, peel and slice. Finely chop pineapple slices. Wash and pat dry rose petals.

3   Heat *ghee* in a pan, add rice and sauté for a few seconds. Add milk

and bring to a boil. Cook till soft. Mash rice with the back of a ladle.

4   Add pumpkin and simmer for five minutes. Add *khoya* and sugar and cook till mixture coats the back of a spoon.  Add rose essence.

5   Remove from heat. Add pineapple and stir. Pour in individual serving bowls and let cool.

6   Garnish with almonds, rose petals and glace cherries. Serve chilled.

# MIXED FRUIT KHEER

## INGREDIENTS

| | | | |
|---|---|---|---|
| Chikoos | 3 | Sugar | 4 tbsps |
| Plums | 3 | Cooked rice | 1¼ cups |
| Pear | 1 | Milk | 5 cups |
| Peaches | 2 | Cornstarch | 1 tbsp |
| Pistachios | 7-8 | Rose syrup | 3 tbsps |
| Butter | 2 tbsps | | |

## METHOD OF PREPARATION

1   Wash chikoos, plums, pear and peaches. Peel, deseed and chop them into half inch sized pieces. Chop pistachios and keep aside for garnish.
2   Heat butter in a pan and sauté fruits for two to three minutes.
3   Add one tablespoon of sugar and cook till sugar melts.
4   Transfer into a serving dish and spread evenly.
5   Add rice to the same pan and sauté. Add more butter if you so wish.

6   Add milk and cook for ten to fifteen minutes or till rice is absolutely soft.
7   Dissolve cornstarch in a little water or milk and add to rice mixture and continue to cook.
8   Add remaining sugar and cook till it dissolves, stirring continuously so it does not stick to the bottom of the pan. Add rose syrup and stir.
9   Pour over sautéed fruits. Sprinkle with pistachios and serve hot or cold.

# TOFFEE APPLE

## INGREDIENTS

| | | |
|---|---|---|
| Apples ................ 4 medium sized | **For the Batter** | |
| Sugar .................................. 1 cup | Refined flour (*maida*) ..... ½ cup | |
| Sesame seeds ..................... 1 tbsp | Cornstarch ........................ 2 tbsps | |
| Oil .............................. to deep fry | Baking powder ................... ½ tsp | |

## METHOD OF PREPARATION

1   To prepare the batter, sift refined flour and cornstarch with baking powder. Slowly stir in one and a quarter cups of water to make a smooth batter. Set it aside for half an hour. Toast sesame seeds lightly and keep aside.

2   Wash, peel, core and cut apples into wedges and dust with flour.

3   Heat sufficient oil in a *kadai*. Dip apple wedges into the batter and deep fry until golden brown. Drain onto an absorbent paper and keep warm.

4   Heat sugar with four tablespoons of water in a thick-bottomed pan,

stirring continuously till sugar dissolves.

5   Continue cooking till it starts caramelizing and becomes pale golden. Remove from heat.

6   Dip apple fritters into hot caramel and then dip immediately in iced water to harden the caramel. (The diners can do this process on the dining table.)

7   Sprinkle toasted sesame seeds on the toffee apple and serve immediately.

# SHRIKHAND

## INGREDIENTS

Yogurt ................................. 3 cups
Sugar (powdered) .......... 2½ cups
Pistachios ............................ 8–10
Sunflower seeds (*charoli*) ... 2 tsps

Milk ................................. 2 tbsps
Saffron ........................ 4-5 strands
Green cardamom powder ... ¼ tsp

## METHOD OF PREPARATION

1   Tie yogurt in a muslin cloth and hang it overnight to drain out the whey. This should be hung in the refrigerator so that the yogurt does not turn sour.

2   Transfer hung yogurt into a bowl. Add powdered sugar and mix well till sugar dissolves completely.

3   Soak pistachios in half a cup of hot water for five to ten minutes. Drain, peel and slice. Clean, wash and pat dry *charoli*.

4   Warm milk slightly and dissolve saffron in it. Add this to the yogurt mixture and mix well.

5   Add *charoli* and green cardamom powder and mix well. Serve chilled, garnished with sliced pistachios.

---

**CHEF'S TIP**

Add one cup of mango puree to this *Shrikhand* to make *Amrakhand,* best enjoyed during summers.

---

# SURTI GHARI

## INGREDIENTS

*Khoya/mawa* (grated) ....2½ cups
Gram flour (*besan*) ............ 2 tsps
Almonds ................................8-10
Sugar (powdered) ............ 6 tbsps
Cashewnuts............................ 7-8

Green cardamom powder... 1 tsp
Refined flour (*maida*) ..........1 cup
*Ghee* ........ 4 tbsps + to deep fry
Sugar ....................................¼ cup

## METHOD OF PREPARATION

1   Blanch, peel and grind almonds to a paste. Grind cashewnuts and keep aside.
2   Heat one tablespoon of *ghee* in a *kadai* and add *besan*. Cook till you start getting the aroma of roasted *besan*. Remove from heat.
3   Add *khoya*, almond paste, powdered sugar, cashewnuts, green cardamom powder and mix well.
4   Dry roast mixture in a *kadai* for two to three minutes. When cool, divide mixture into equal portions.

5   Sieve *maida*. Knead into a stiff dough using water as required. Leave it covered for one hour. Add one tablespoon of *ghee* and knead again.

6   Divide in equal portions and roll them out very thinly. Stuff them with *khoya* mixture and roll into a round ball. Flatten slightly on the top and the edges to give it a pellet shape.

7   Heat sufficient *ghee* in a *kadai* and deep-fry the *gharis* on very low heat till light golden. This may take fifteen to twenty minutes. Remove when it turns golden brown.

8   Take some cold water in a *handi*. Heat two tablespoons of *ghee* in a separate but smaller *handi*. Place it in the *handi* containing the cold water and cool the *ghee* stirring constantly so that it is smooth when cold but not set. Add powdered sugar and mix well.

9   Dip the *ghari* in the *ghee* and remove. Place it on the wire rack so that excess *ghee* drains out.

10  Store in airtight tins with butter paper placed between the *gharis*.

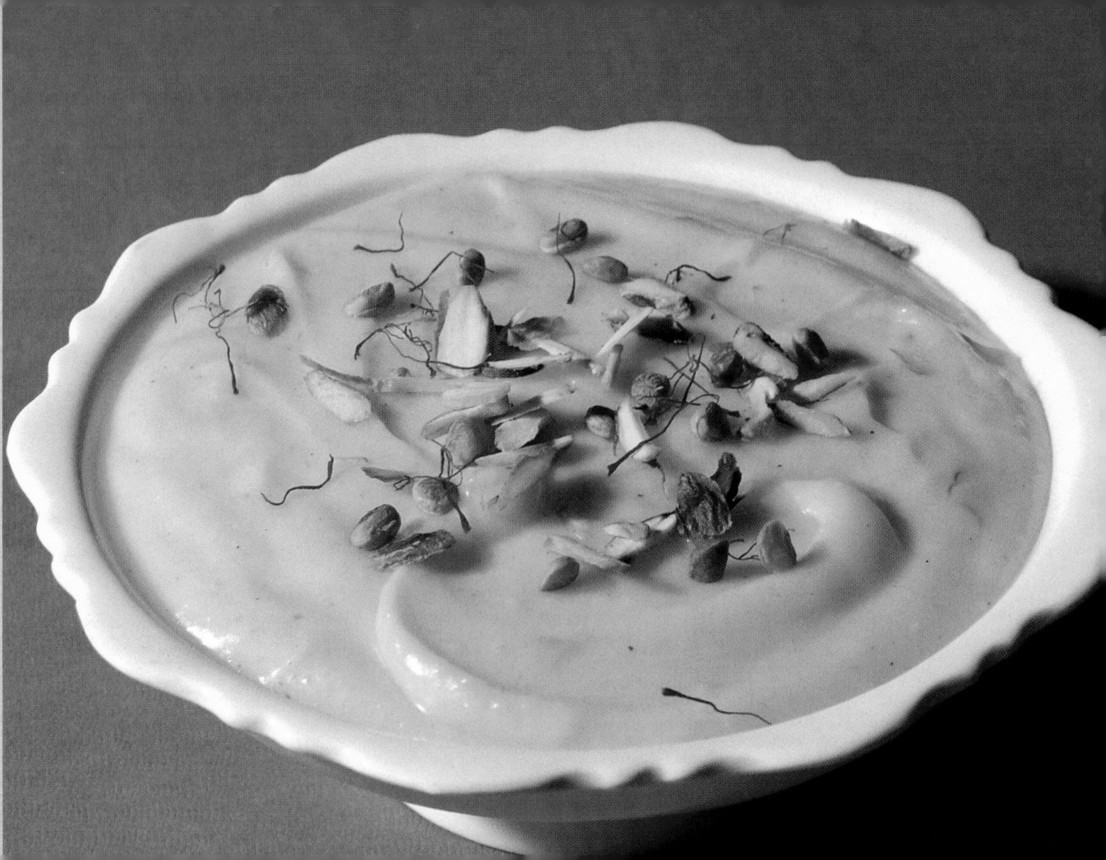

Shrikhand

Strawberry and Pista Phirni

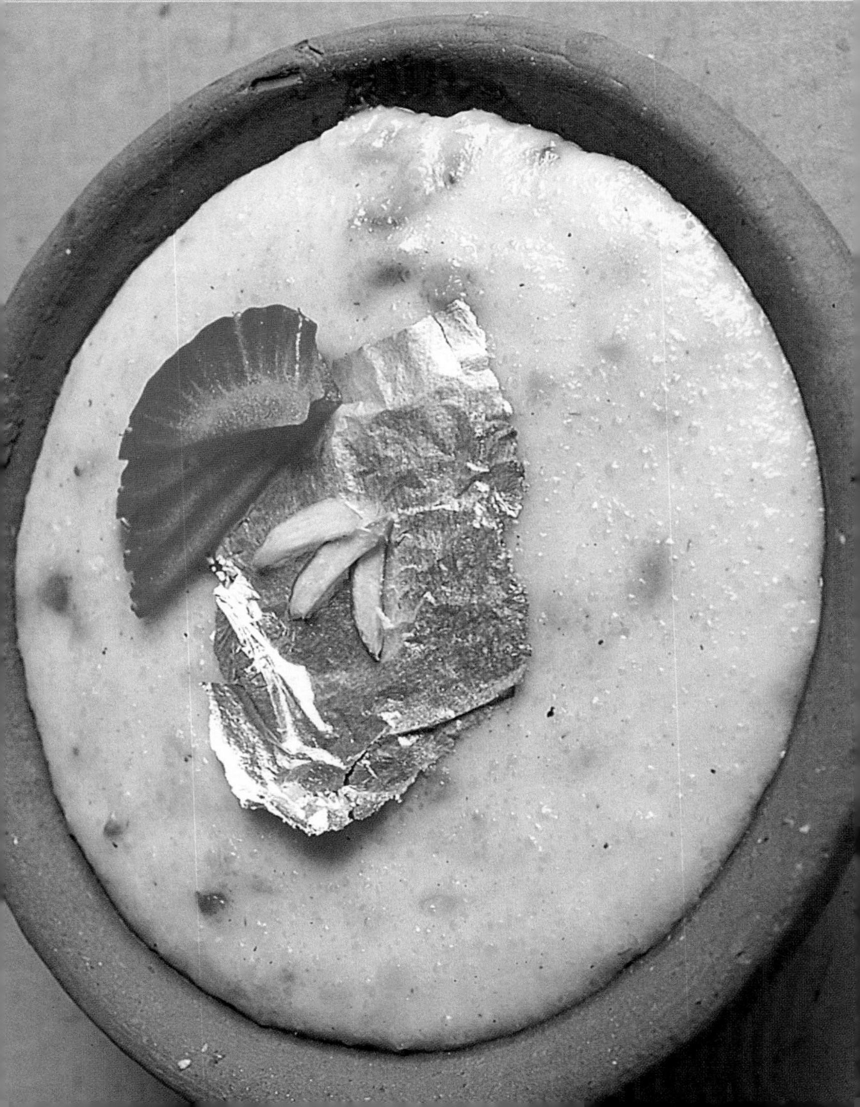

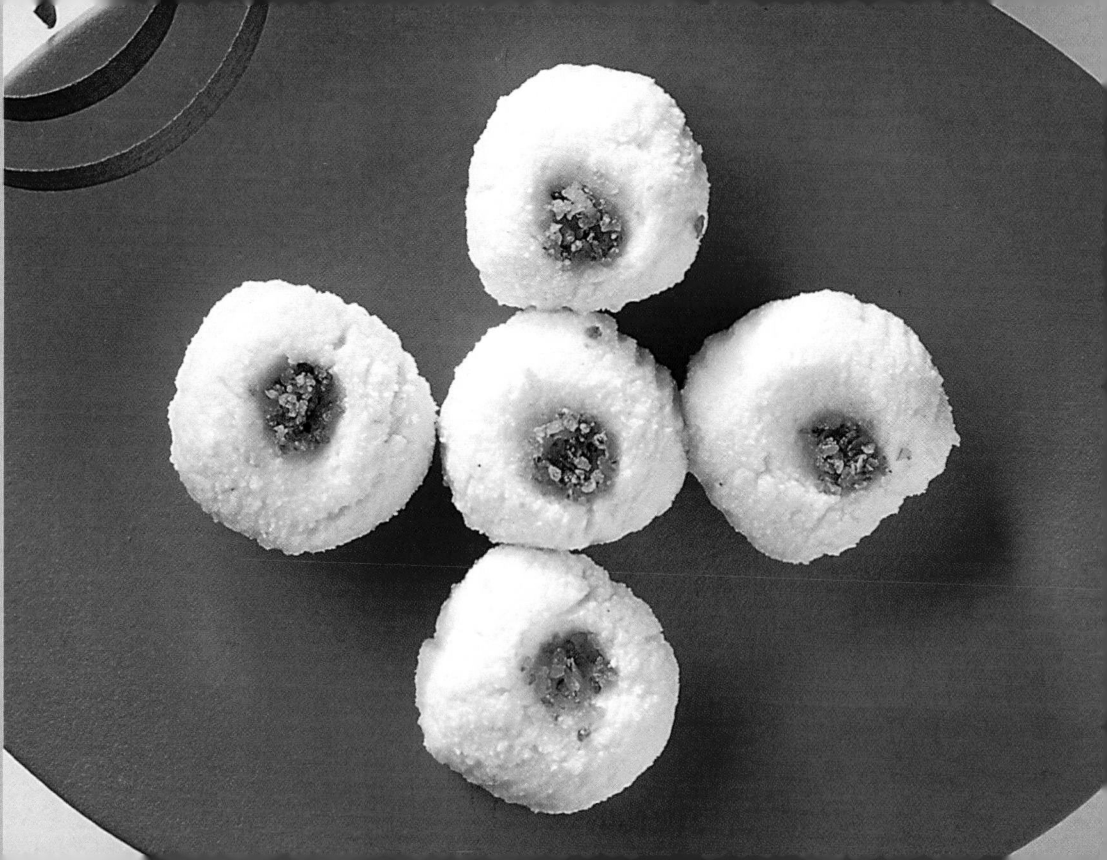

Sandesh

# SANDESH

## INGREDIENTS

| | | | |
|---|---|---|---|
| Fresh *Chenna* | 2 cups | Almonds | 10-12 |
| Sugar (powdered) | ½ cup | Saffron | 7-8 strands |
| Green cardamom powder | ½ tsp | Warm milk | 1 tbsp |
| Pistachios | 8-10 | | |

## METHOD OF PREPARATION

1. Soak pistachios and almonds in one cup of hot water for ten minutes. Drain, peel and chop them separately. Lightly crush and dissolve saffron in warm milk. Mix chopped pistachios in milk and saffron mixture.
2. Knead *chenna* with your palm to ensure a smooth texture. Add powdered sugar and green cardamom powder and knead well.
3. Transfer mixture into a *kadai* and cook on low heat for five to six minutes, stirring continuously. Remove from heat, mix gently till it is cool enough to handle.
4. Mix in almonds and divide into twenty equal portions.
5. Form each portion into desired shape, garnish with chopped pistachios and soaked saffron. Chill thoroughly and serve.

> **CHEF'S TIP**
> Since *Sandesh* has a short shelf life, it is recommended that it be consumed on the same day.

# STRAWBERRY AND PISTA PHIRNI

## INGREDIENTS

Fresh strawberries .... 12-15 small sized
Rice ................................. 4 tbsps
Pistachios ........................... 8-10
Almonds .............................. 6-8
Milk ................................. 4 cups
Sugar ................................. ¾ cup
Green cardamom powder ... ½ tsp

## METHOD OF PREPARATION

1   Clean, wash and soak rice in sufficient water for half an hour. Drain and grind soaked rice to a coarse paste. Dilute rice paste with half a cup of water.
2   Wash and hull strawberries. Slice two of them and keep aside for garnishing. Finely chop the remaining.
3   Soak pistachios and almonds in hot water for five minutes. Drain, peel and slice finely.

4   Heat milk in a pan and bring it to a boil. Gradually stir in rice paste. Reduce heat and simmer for three to four minutes, stirring continuously or till milk thickens.

5   Add sugar, cardamom powder and continue to simmer till sugar dissolves and is incorporated well. Remove from heat, cool to room temperature and stir in chopped strawberries.

6   Pour this mixture into individual earthenware or ceramic bowls, garnish with sliced pistachios, almonds and strawberry slices and serve chilled.

# RASMALAI

## INGREDIENTS

| | |
|---|---|
| Chenna ................... 1 ½ cups | Sugar ................................. 4 cups |
| Refined flour (maida) ..... 4 tbsps | Milk ................................... 10 cups |
| Pistachios ........................... 10-12 | |

## METHOD OF PREPARATION

1  Crumble *chenna* and mash it. Add two tablespoons of *maida* and knead with the palm of your hand to make a smooth dough.
2  Divide into sixteen equal portions. Roll into balls and press slightly to flatten them.
3  Blanch pistachios in hot water. Cool, remove skin and slice.
4  Dissolve two cups of sugar in the same quantity of water, bring to a boil and add the rest of the *maida* dissolved in a little water.
5  Slowly lower *chenna* balls in the boiling syrup and cook on high heat for ten minutes. Add half a cup of water and bring to a boil again. Cook for three minutes.

6  Meanwhile prepare a thin sugar syrup with one cup of sugar and two cups of water.

7  Soak cooked *chenna* balls in this syrup.

8  Boil milk in a thick-bottomed pan, lower heat and continue to boil till it is reduced to a thick consistency.

9  Add the rest of the sugar and keep boiling till sugar dissolves. Remove from heat, cool and refrigerate for an hour.

10 Squeeze *chenna* balls and put them into the chilled milk. Refrigerate it for another half an hour.

11 Serve chilled garnished with pistachios.

**CHEF'S TIP**

Use *chenna* made from cow's milk. Best *chenna* is made by curdling cow's milk with leftover *whey* of *chenna* made earlier. The trick lies in curdling and the acid content should be just right, if it were too much, the *chenna* would become tough.

# SUJI AUR BADAM KA HALWA

## INGREDIENTS

Semolina (*rawa/ suji*) ......... 1 cup
Almonds ........................ 2½ cups
Ghee ............................... ½ cup
Sugar .............................. 2½ cups

Milk ...................................... 1 cup
Saffron ........................ few strands
Green cardamom powder .. 1½ tsps

## METHOD OF PREPARATION

1   Heat a pan and dry roast semolina.
2   Blanch almonds, peel and pat them dry. Grind to a coarse powder.
3   Heat *ghee* in a pan, add almond powder and sauté over medium heat till golden.
4   Add semolina and mix well.
5   Add sugar and mix. Add milk and stir to mix well. Let it cook for eight to ten minutes.

6 Add saffron and stir. Continue to cook till the *halwa* thickens.
7 Add green cardamom powder and stir to mix well.
8 Add one tablespoon of *ghee* to finish off and serve hot.

# MATAR KI KHEER

## INGREDIENTS

Green peas (shelled) ......... 1 cup
Raisins ................................ 20-25
Pistachios ......................... 20-25
*Ghee* ............................... ½ cup

Milk ................................ 6 ½ cups
Sugar ................................ 1 cup
Green cardamom powder... 1 tsp

## METHOD OF PREPARATION

1  Wash and boil green peas for five minutes. Refresh in cold water and grind to a fine paste.
2  Wash raisins and pat them dry. Thinly slice pistachios.
3  Heat *ghee* in a thick-bottomed pan, add green peas paste and cook for a few minutes, stirring continuously. Keep aside.
4  Boil milk in a pan and add to cooked green peas paste. Bring it to a boil. Cook on low heat for fifteen to twenty minutes or till the milk is reduced to half.
5  Add sugar, green cardamom powder, raisins and sliced pistachios. Cook for about eight to ten minutes on low heat, stirring continuously. Remove from heat and allow it to cool. Chill in refrigerator. Serve cold.

*Amrakhand*

# AMRAKHAND

## INGREDIENTS

Yogurt ................................... 2 cups

Condensed milk ............... ¾ cup

Mango puree .................... ½ cup

Mango essence .................... ½ tsp

Sunflower seeds (*charoli*) ..... 1 tsp

## METHOD OF PREPARATION

1  Put yogurt in a muslin cloth and hang it for one hour to drain away excess whey. Press to make sure all the excess water is removed.
2  Blend with condensed milk, mango puree and essence in a blender to make it smooth.
3  Sprinkle sunflower seeds and chill till almost frozen. Serve cold.

# PEAS AND PRUNES
# KHEER

## INGREDIENTS

| | | | |
|---|---|---|---|
| Green peas (shelled) ........ ¾ cup | | *Ghee* ........................... ¼ cup |
| Prunes ................................ ½ cup | | Milk ..................................... 5 cups |
| Raisins ................................ 20-25 | | Bread slices ................................ 2 |
| Rose petals ...................... 10 - 12 | | Sugar .................................... ½ cup |
| Pistachios ........................... 20-25 | | Green cardamom powder ... 1 tsp |

## METHOD OF PREPARATION

1   Wash and boil green peas for five minutes. Refresh in cold water and grind to a fine paste.

2   Wash prunes and remove seeds. Stew them in a cup of hot water for ten minutes. Roughly chop and keep aside. Wash and pat dry raisins and rose petals. Slice pistachios.

3   Heat *ghee* in a thick-bottomed pan, add green peas paste and cook for a few minutes, stirring continuously. Keep aside.

4   Boil milk with rose petals. Simmer for ten minutes on low heat and strain the milk.

5   Add milk to prepared green peas paste. Bring to a boil. Cook on low heat for fifteen to twenty minutes or till milk is reduced to half.

6   Trim the edges of bread slices. Discard edges. Soak bread slices in water. Squeeze out the water completely and add this to the milk and peas mixture. Mix well.

7   Add sugar, green cardamom powder and raisins. Cook for about ten minutes on low heat. Take off the heat and set aside to cool.

8   Add prunes to the cooled peas *kheer* and serve chilled topped with sliced pistachios.

# SEMIYA PAYASAM

## INGREDIENTS

| | | | |
|---|---|---|---|
| Vermicelli (*semiya*) | 1 cup | Green cardamoms | 4 |
| Pure *ghee* | 2 tbsps | Sugar | 1½ cups |
| Milk | 2 cups | Saffron | a generous pinch |
| Cashewnuts | 12 | Nutmeg powder | ¼ tsp |

## METHOD OF PREPARATION

1 Heat *ghee* in a pan, add vermicelli and cashewnuts and fry till a pleasant aroma is released.
2 Grind cardamoms with little sugar to a fine powder.
3 Boil milk in a thick-bottomed pan, and add to the roasted vermicelli and cashewnuts. Mix well and simmer for five minutes.
4 Add sugar and continue cooking, stirring continuously.
5 Cook for three to four minutes or till it thickens to the right consistency. Sprinkle saffron, cardamom and nutmeg powder.
6 Stir well and serve as desired – hot, warm or chilled.

# STEAMED DATE BUNS

## INGREDIENTS

### Dough
Refined flour (*maida*) .... 2½ cups
Sugar ..................................... 3 tsps
Milk ....................................... ½ cup
Dry yeast ......................... 1½ tbsps
Salt ......................................... ¼ tsp
Sesame oil ........................... 1 tbsp

### Filling
Seedless dates ...................... ½ cup
Walnut kernels ................... ½ cup
Butter ................................... 1 tbsp
Sweet bean paste ............. 2 tbsps

## METHOD OF PREPARATION

1 Dissolve sugar and dry yeast in lukewarm milk and leave aside for fifteen minutes or until frothy. Sieve refined flour and salt together. Make a well in the center, add yeast mixture and make a soft dough using water as needed.

2 Add sesame oil and knead dough with your palm and leave aside in a warm place for fifteen minutes or until it doubles in size. Knock

out the air bubbles by kneading once again and divide into sixteen equal portions.

3  Clean and finely chop dates. Wipe and roughly chop walnuts.

4  Heat butter in a pan and stir in bean paste diluted in two tablespoons of water.

5  Add dates and cook for two minutes till it starts leaving the sides of the pan. Remove from heat and cool.

6  Roll each portion of the dough into two inch round discs, place a portion of the filling and gather the sides to form into a ball.

7  Rest prepared buns covered with a moist cloth for five minutes. Place in bamboo steamers and steam on high heat for fifteen minutes or until completely cooked. Serve hot straight from the steamer.

# BURFIWALI
# CHOCOLATE PHIRNI

## INGREDIENTS

| | | | |
|---|---|---|---|
| Rice | 5 tbsps | Cocoa powder | ¼ cup |
| Pistachios | 4-5 | Sugar | ¾ cup |
| Milk | 5 cups | *Kaju katli* | 10 |

## METHOD OF PREPARATION

1  Pick, wash and soak rice in one and half cups of water for half an hour and grind to a coarse paste. Blanch pistachios in half a cup of hot water. Drain, peel and slice.
2  Bring milk to a boil. Mix cocoa in a little cold milk and add to the boiling milk.
3  Add rice paste and cook till it is a little thick.
4  Add sugar and cook till it dissolves.
5  Cut *kaju katli* into cubes and add to the *phirni*.
6  Pour into an earthenware pot. Sprinkle sliced *pistachios* and let *phirni* cool.
7  Serve chilled.

# MAWA GUJIYA

## INGREDIENTS

**For outer covering**
Refined flour (*maida*) ....... 4 cups
Ghee ........ 5 tbsps + to deep fry
**For Filling**
*Khoya/mawa* (grated) ...2 ½ cups
Almonds .................................. 15
Cashewnuts............................. 15

Raisins ...................................... 20
Chocolate ............................... ½ cup
Desiccated coconut........ 3¼ tsps
Nutmeg powder .............. a pinch
Green cardamom powder.. ¼ tsp
Sugar (powdered) .......... 2½ cups

## METHOD OF PREPARATION

1  For preparing the covering, sieve flour and rub in five tablespoons of *ghee*. Add cold water and knead into a soft dough. Cover it with a moist cloth and keep aside.
2  Roast *khoya* in a deep pan on medium heat till pink. Remove from heat, transfer into a bowl and let it cool.
3  Soak almonds in half a cup of hot water for ten minutes. Drain,

    peel and chop them. Chop cashewnuts. Wash and pat dry raisins. Grate chocolate.

4    Add desiccated coconut, cashewnuts, almonds, raisins, nutmeg powder, green cardamom powder to *khoya* and mix well.

5    Add powdered sugar and grated chocolate and mix properly.

6    With oiled hands divide dough into small balls. Grease the *gujia* mould.

7    Roll out dough balls into small *puris*, put it on the mould and press lightly. Place the stuffing in the hollow portion. Apply a little water on the edges, close mould and press firmly.

8    Open mould and remove extra dough. Keep *gujias* covered with a damp cloth. Similarly use up all the dough and stuffing.

9    If you do not have a mould, *gujias* can still be prepared. Roll out *puris*, cut with a *katori* to get a proper round shape. Place stuffing on one half, lightly dampen edges and fold the other half over the stuffing and press edges firmly using a fork.

10    Heat sufficient oil in a *kadai* and deep fry *gujias* on medium heat till golden brown.

11    Let it cool slightly before serving, as the stuffing inside may be very hot.

# RICE KHEER

### INGREDIENTS

Basmati rice ...................... 3 tbsps
Whole cream milk ............ 5 cups
Sugar .................................. 6 tbsps
Cashewnuts ........................ 10-12
Raisins ................................. 12-14
Green cardamoms ................. 5-6
Saffron ........................ 6-8 strands

### METHOD OF PREPARATION

1   Pick, wash and soak rice for two hours in one cup of water. Drain and keep aside. Chop cashewnuts. Wash and pat dry raisins. Peel and powder cardamoms. Soak saffron strands in one tablespoon of warm milk.
2   Heat milk in a pan and bring to a boil, add rice and reduce heat.
3   Cook, stirring continuously, till it reduces to one-third of the original quantity.
4   Add sugar and mix well by partially crushing rice.
5   Add cardamom powder, saffron milk, cashewnuts and raisins. Serve hot or cold.

# ORANGE RICE PUDDING

## INGREDIENTS

Rice .................................... 1/3 cup
Skimmed milk ................... 2 cups
Raisins ................................ ½ cup
Dates (seedless) ...................... 6-8

Honey ............................ 1½ tbsps
Vanilla essence .................... ¼ tsp
Orange rind (grated) ........... 1 tsp
Fresh orange juice ............. ½ cup

## METHOD OF PREPARATION

1  Pick, wash and soak rice in one cup of water for half an hour. Drain and keep aside. Soak raisins in one cup of water for fifteen minutes. Squeeze out excess water. Chop dates roughly.

2  Boil milk in a non-stick saucepan. Add rice to the boiling milk, reduce heat and cook, stirring continuously till rice is soft and milk is completely absorbed. Remove from heat and cool to room temperature. Preheat oven to 160°C.

3  Combine cooked rice with honey, raisins, vanilla essence, dates, orange rind and fresh orange juice.

4  Pour into a medium sized ceramic or glass ovenproof dish. Bake in the preheated oven at 160°C for fifteen minutes. Serve warm or chilled.

# CHOCOLATE
# BROWNIES

## INGREDIENTS

Refined flour *(maida)* ...... 1 cup

Powdered sugar ................. ¾ cup

Dark chocolate (melted) .... ¼ cup

Baking powder ................... ¾ tsp

Soda bicarbonate ............... ¾ tsp

Butter (melted) ................. ¼ cup

Vanilla essence ................... ½ tsp

## METHOD OF PREPARATION

1  Preheat oven to 180°C.  Greased and dust a five inch cake tin.
2  Sieve together flour, powdered sugar, baking powder and soda bicarbonate into a bowl.
3  In another bowl mix melted dark chocolate, melted butter and vanilla essence.
4  Add the flour mixture to the chocolate mixture gradually and mix well.

5    Transfer the batter into the prepared tin and bake in the preheated oven at 180°C for fifty to fifty minutes.
6    Shift onto a wire rack to cool before cutting into slices to serve.

# GAJAR HALWA

## INGREDIENTS

| | |
|---|---|
| Carrots ......... 8-10 medium sized | Milk ...................................... 2 cups |
| Cashewnuts ............................. 5-6 | Green cardamom powder .. ¼ tsp |
| Almonds ................................. 5-6 | *Khoya/mawa* (grated) ........ 1 cup |
| Raisins ................................. 10-15 | Sugar ...................................... ¾ cup |
| Pure *ghee* .................... 3 tbsps | Silver *varq* .................. 1 sheet |

## METHOD OF PREPARATION

1  Peel, wash and grate carrots. Chop cashewnuts. Blanch almonds in half a cup of hot water for five minutes. Drain, cool, peel and slice them. Wash raisins and pat them dry.

2  Heat pure *ghee* in a thick-bottomed pan, add grated carrots and sauté for five minutes.

3  Add milk, green cardamom powder and cook on medium heat for five to six minutes or till milk evaporates and carrots are cooked.

4  Stir in *khoya* and sugar and cook for two to three minutes or till sugar melts and mixes well, stirring continuously. Continue to cook for two minutes more.

5  Garnish with cashewnuts, almonds and raisins. Decorate with silver *varq*. Serve hot or at room temperature.

# GULAB JAMUN

## INGREDIENTS

*Khoya/mawa* ............... 1½ cups
*Chenna (paneer)* ............ ¼ cup
Soda bicarbonate ............... ¼ tsp
Refined flour *(maida)* ..... 3 tbsps

Green cardamom powder .. ¼ tsp
Sugar ................................... 2 cups
*Ghee*/oil ........................ to deep fry

## METHOD OF PREPARATION

1   Grate *khoya*, mash *chenna* and keep them aside.
2   Mix the two along with soda bicarbonate, refined flour, green
    cardamom powder and a little water to make a soft dough.
3   Divide into sixteen equal portions and shape into balls.
4   To prepare a sugar syrup, heat two cups of water and add sugar to
    it. Stir to dissolve the sugar. Clear the syrup by removing the scum,
    if any.
5   Heat sufficient *ghee*/oil in a *kadai*.  Add the balls and deep fry on

low heat till golden in colour. Drain them onto an absorbent kitchen towel or paper.

6   Soak the fried balls in the sugar syrup for atleast fifteen to twenty minutes before serving.

CHEF'S TIP

Temperature of the oil should be low or the *jamuns* will remain uncooked from inside. You may stuff *Gulab Jamuns* with saffron and pistachio nuts or *mishri*.

Gulab Jamun

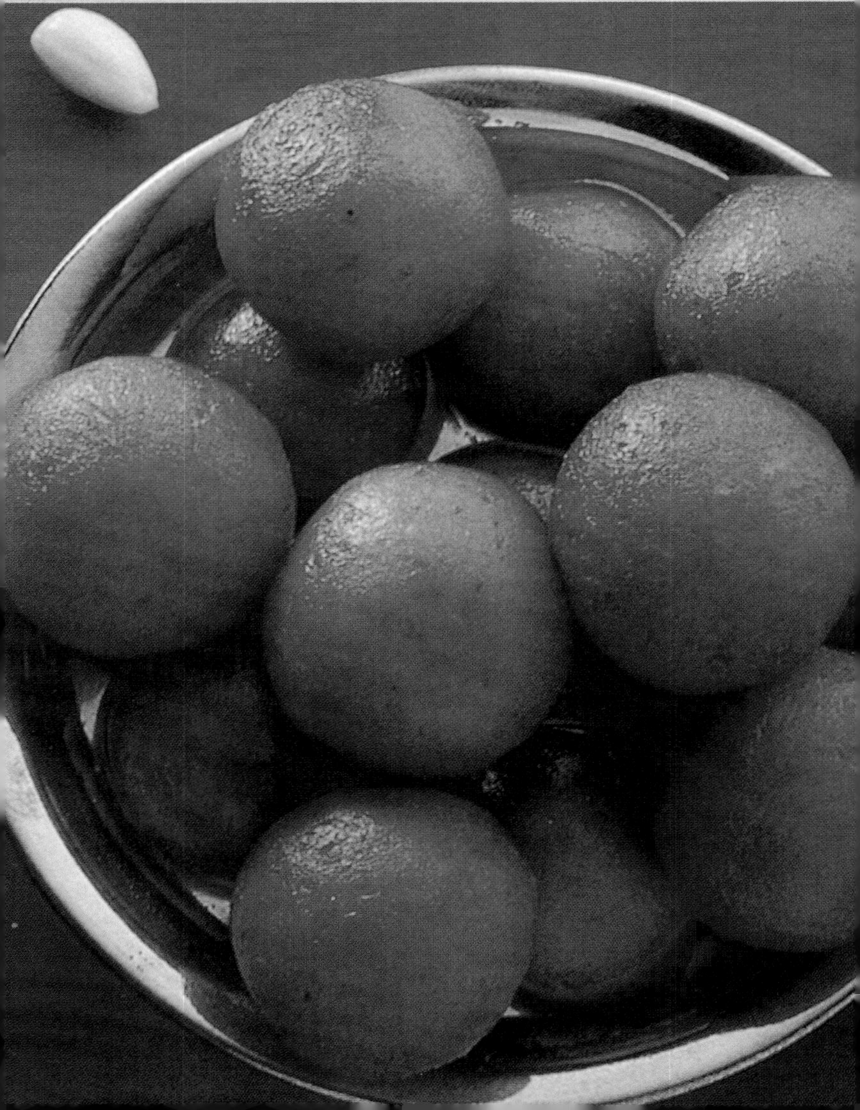

Chocolate Brownies

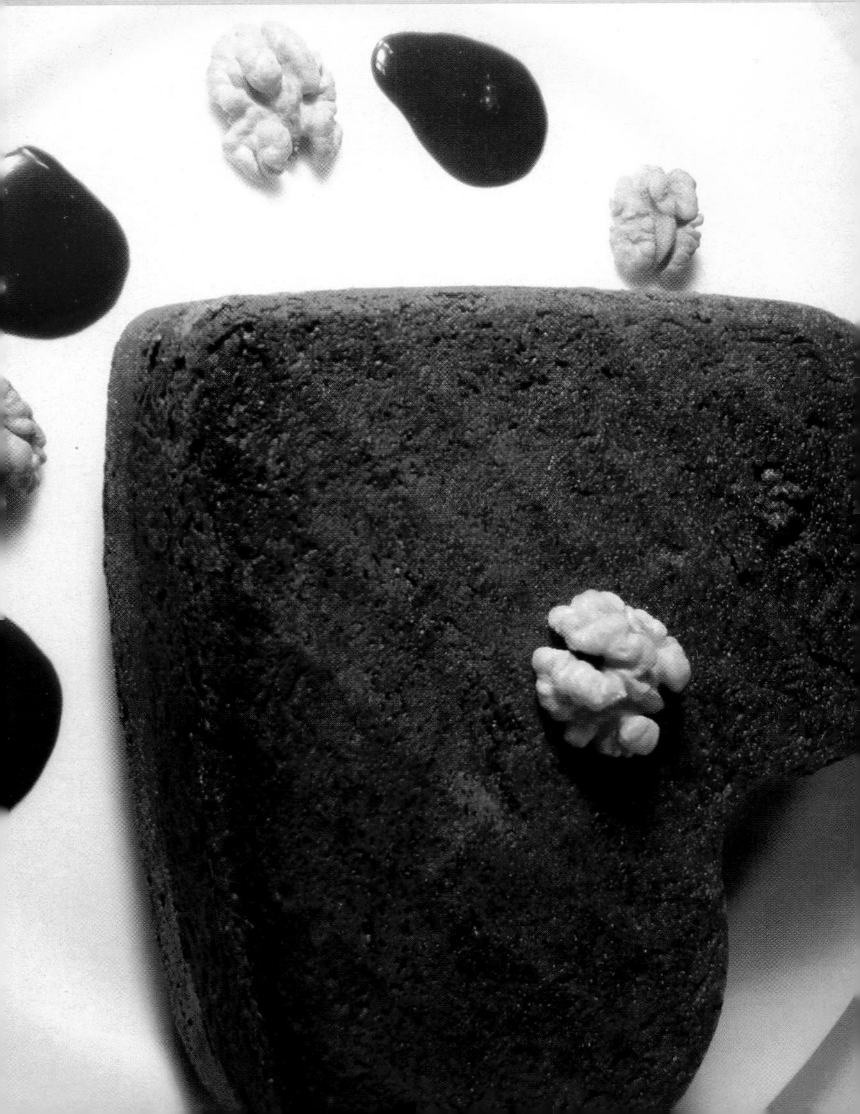